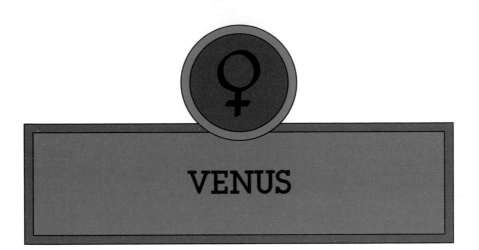

VENUS

MURIEL SCHLOSS

VENUS

A FIRST BOOK
FRANKLIN WATTS
NEW YORK/LONDON/TORONTO/SYDNEY/1991

To my family, especially
Brian, who is already on his way,
and
Graham, who is just beginning

Cover photographs courtesy of: NASA

All photographs courtesy of
NASA except: Sovfoto/Tass:
pp. 24, 25; NASA U.S.
Geological Survey: pp. 30, 31.

Library of Congress Cataloging-in-Publication Data

Schloss, Muriel.
    Venus / by Muriel Schloss.
    p. cm. — (A First book)
    Includes bibliographical references and index
    Summary: Uses photographs and other recent findings to describe,
the atmosphere and geographic features of Venus.
    ISBN 0-531-20019-1 (lib. bdg.)—ISBN 0-531-15772-5 (pbk.)
    1. Venus (Planet)—Juvenile literature. [1. Venus (Planet)]
I. Title. II. Series.
QB621.S38 1991
623.4'2—dc20   90-13101 CIP AC

CONTENTS

ACKNOWLEDGMENTS

To the many people who have helped me in the preparation of this book—thank you very much!

Especially Dr. R. Stephen Saunders, Jet Propulsion Laboratory, Pasadena, California, project scientist, who leads science activities for the radar exploration of Venus—for the generous gift of his time, patience, and expertise, and for graciously editing the factual content of this book; Dr. E. Richard Cohen, Distinguished Fellow, Rockwell International, Los Angeles, California—for his interest and meticulous attention to detail; Robert Mullen, Hughes Aircraft Company, El Segundo, California, Radar Project Manager who introduced me to *Magellan* and the incredible SAR; NASA's William Piotrowski, JPL's John Gerpheide,

William T. K. Johnson, and Jim Doyle for providing me with excellent information and the answers to my endless questions; Brian Heimberg, whose curiosity inspired me and kept me going; Harriette Abels for her friendship, encouragement, and guidance; Lou Schloss, Libby Atwater, Barbara Hopfinger, Maryon Lears, Bud Lesser, and Carolyn Zucker for giving unstintingly of their time, advice, and support; Elsie Neugarten, my "volunteer" proofreader; and Carolynn Young for her suggestions and essential verifications.

BRIGHT TORCH OF HEAVEN

CHAPTER ONE

"Pirates!" the lookout shouted. "Port quarter! Bearing ten miles!"

Lumbering through brisk mid-Atlantic waters, the homeward bound crew of a treasure-laden Spanish galleon doused the ship's oil lamps. All hands scurried to their stations. Sweating and tense, 350 men stared through the darkness, eyes glued to a brilliant light shining on the western horizon.

Even though sailors in the 1500s charted their courses by the stars, the planet Venus often fooled them. When it appeared low in the evening sky, it seemed to sit on the water waiting, like a pirate ship, ready to pounce.

Many sailors actually shot their guns at Venus.

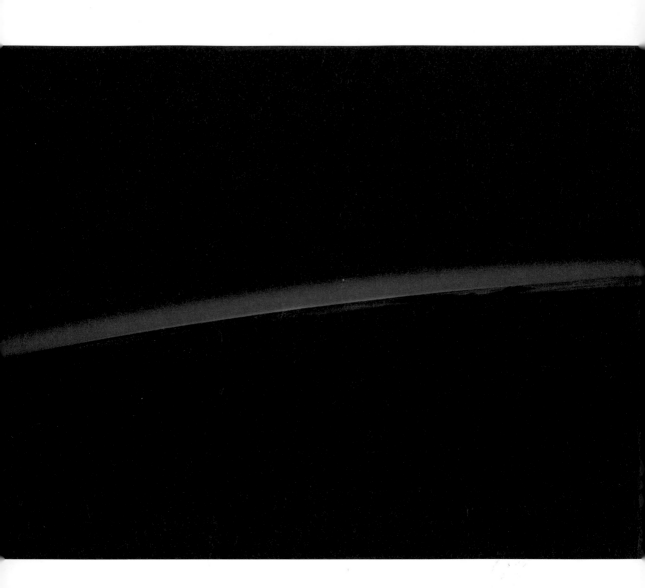

Venus appears as a white speck on the
horizon in this sunset scene taken high above
the Earth by the space shuttle *Atlantis*.

10

Astronomers and scientists still "shoot" at it with *radar* telescopes, probes, and unmanned spacecraft.

None of these give experts as much information as they want, however. Only three land-based radar telescopes can see through the dense clouds that blanket Venus. Probes last less than an hour in the planet's furnacelike heat and crushing pressure. Unmanned spacecraft, including America's *Pioneer Venus,* which has been orbiting the planet since 1978, have sent back only hazy images of the Venusian surface.

VENUS: EARTH'S NEAREST NEIGHBOR

Venus is Earth's nearest neighbor. The two are often called planetary "twins" because they have so many similarities. Both were formed about 4½ billion years ago. Both have solid surfaces, and are practically the same in size and in density.

Dr. R. Stephen Saunders, project scientist at the Jet Propulsion Laboratory (JPL) in Pasadena, California, who leads science activities for the radar exploration of Venus, says that, "If you ground up both of the planets with a big mortar and pestle, you would find they had nearly identical composition."

These likenesses only make scientists more curious. They want to know:

1. Why have the two planets developed so differently?
2. Was there ever any kind of life on Venus?
3. Did the planet ever have water?
4. Does it have *tectonic* activity (the movements of a system of *plates* that lie beneath the planet's surface)?

RUNAWAY GREENHOUSE

Scientists also want to know: Why has Venus become so hot it cannot cool off? What caused its atmosphere to retain so many poisonous gases? What made it become a "runaway greenhouse"?

The *Magellan* spacecraft is released from the space shuttle *Atlantis* on May 4, 1989, to begin its fifteen-month journey to Venus. Its cloud-piercing radar is designed to map the Venusian surface.

A greenhouse is a glass house used for growing plants. Glass lets the sun's rays in to warm the greenhouse, but it also traps the heat so it cannot get out. This causes the greenhouse to get hotter and hotter.

Venus's clouds are like the glass. The heat can get in but it cannot get out. Now Venus is so hot that scientists call it a runaway greenhouse.

In the past century, Earth has also gotten warmer. Does that mean Earth will become a runaway greenhouse? How can we prevent that from happening?

Experts believe the *Magellan* spacecraft, with its special cloud-piercing radar, will answer some of their questions. The radar bounces signals off the Venusian surface, transmits them back to Earth, and tells investigators what the surface

Venus's dense atmosphere has caused a "runaway greenhouse" effect on the planet. The clouds rotate around the planet once every four days.

looks like. From that, experts hope to discover how Venus was formed and how it got to be the way it is.

EARLY BELIEFS

Thousands of years ago, ancient people tried to understand what the stars and their movements meant. They saw that night after night and year after year, many of the stars traveled in groups. The ancients named those groups constellations.

There were, however, a few stars that behaved independently. Each moved across the sky at its own speed. Each traveled in its own great sweeping path or circle, called an orbit. Astronomers named those stars planets—from the Greek word *planete* meaning "wanderer."

Venus is a wanderer. It is the brightest of all nine planets in the solar system. Its silvery brilliance comes from the Sun's reflection off the planet's clouds.

Long ago, ancients thought the solar system consisted of the Sun, the Moon, and only five planets. Earth was not considered a planet. It was believed to be the center of the universe.

In those days, people believed that the planets represented some of the gods and goddesses they worshiped. The people chose symbols to represent their favorite gods and designated days of the week to honor them.

Mars was named after the god of war, because of its angry red color. Jupiter, the largest planet, honored the king of the gods. And one planet was called Mercury because, like the fleet-footed messenger of those ancient gods, it moved so rapidly across the sky.

Venus was special. It was the only planet named for a woman. Because of its dazzling light, both the Greeks and Romans named it after their goddesses of love and beauty. The Greeks named it Aphrodite, the Romans Venus.

The Chinese called Venus Tai-pe, which means "beautiful white one." The Babylonians called it Ishtar, "the bright torch of heaven." Sometimes that torch shone so brightly, it even cast shadows on the Earth.

In the seven-day week, Venus was assigned the sixth day. "Venus's day," translates into *venerdi* in Italian, *viernes* in Spanish, and *vendredi* in French. In English, the sixth day of the week is Friday; in German it is *Freitag*. Both honor Freia, the Norse goddess of love and beauty.

Because of its beauty, the ancients designed a symbol like a hand mirror to represent Venus. Today, that hand mirror symbol represents the female sex.

The crescent of Venus, as seen
from *Pioneer Venus*

18

ANCIENT ASTRONOMERS

For centuries, ancient astronomers thought of Venus as two stars. When they saw it in the morning, in the eastern sky, they called it Phosphoros. When they saw it in the evening, in the western sky, they called it Hesperos. As generations of astronomers watched Venus appear and disappear, they began to understand its cycle. But it was Pythagoras of Samos (582 B.C.–507 B.C.) who is said to have discovered that the morning star and the evening star were one.

Centuries later, in the 1600s, the Italian scientist Galileo used his telescope to study the stars. One of his findings was so shocking that it took twenty years before he gathered enough courage to publish a paper about it.

At that time, most people believed Earth was the center of the solar system and that the planets revolved around it. So Galileo expected to see a full or a three-quarter Venus. What he did see were only crescent shapes. Because the crescents seemed sometimes larger, sometimes smaller, Galileo called them the *phases of Venus.* They proved to him that Venus orbited not the Earth, but the Sun.

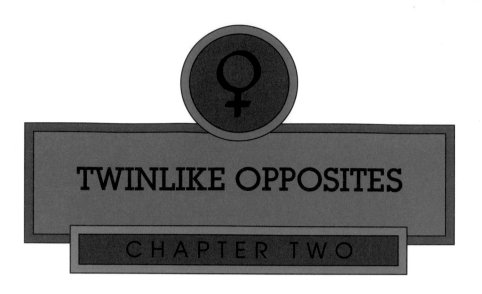

TWINLIKE OPPOSITES

CHAPTER TWO

Over the centuries, people have invented stories about bright, beautiful, mysterious Venus. Some imagined that Venus was a paradise, others that it was covered by a petroleum ocean. Still others were just as certain that exotic animals roamed swamps and forests on its surface.

During World War II, scientists developed a tool called radar, for RAdio Detection And Ranging. At first it was used to locate enemy airplanes. Eventually it helped astronomers learn more about Venus.

In 1962, America's unmanned spacecraft, *Mariner 2,* flew past Venus. Soaring 22,000 miles above the Venusian clouds, *Mariner 2* measured the planet's temperature. The results not only confirmed earlier radar readings of 625°F, but added to them. Venus's surface temperature was actually 890°F—hot enough to boil mercury and to melt tin and lead.

By 1978, three U.S. land-based telescopes had their radar beams trained on Venus. America's *Pioneer Venus* spacecraft, with its simple radar, orbited the planet. And scientists waited excitedly for information they thought would help them solve the mystery of Earth's sister planet.

VENUS: MYSTERIES

What scientists learned raised new questions, such as, why does Venus turn from east to west on its *axis*?

An axis is an imaginary line between a planet's north and south poles. Using that imaginary line, scientists can tell the direction in which a planet revolves, or turns. Scientists say that on Venus, the Sun rises in the west and sets in the east. That is the opposite direction, *retrograde,* from the way Earth and all the other planets in the solar system turn. Only in 1989 did astronomers find another celestial body that turned the same way. It was not a planet, but one of Neptune's moons, Triton.

Scientists also found that a single Venusian day lasts longer than a Venusian year. Venus whirls around the Sun in 225 Earth days. But, it takes 18 days longer, 243 Earth days, for the planet to make one complete turn on its axis.

Since 1978, *Pioneer Venus* has sent back *data,* or information, about the planet and its *gravity.* Gravity is an unseen power that pulls objects toward the planet nearest to it. Each planet, including the Sun, has its own area or *field of gravity.* We keep our feet on the ground, apples fall down out of trees instead of up, and the Moon circles our planet, all because of the strong pull of Earth's gravity.

In this computer-enhanced image of the Venusian atmosphere, darker areas represent sulfur and sulfur dioxide and lighter ones, sulfuric acid. High concentrations of sulfur dioxide may indicate volcanic activity.

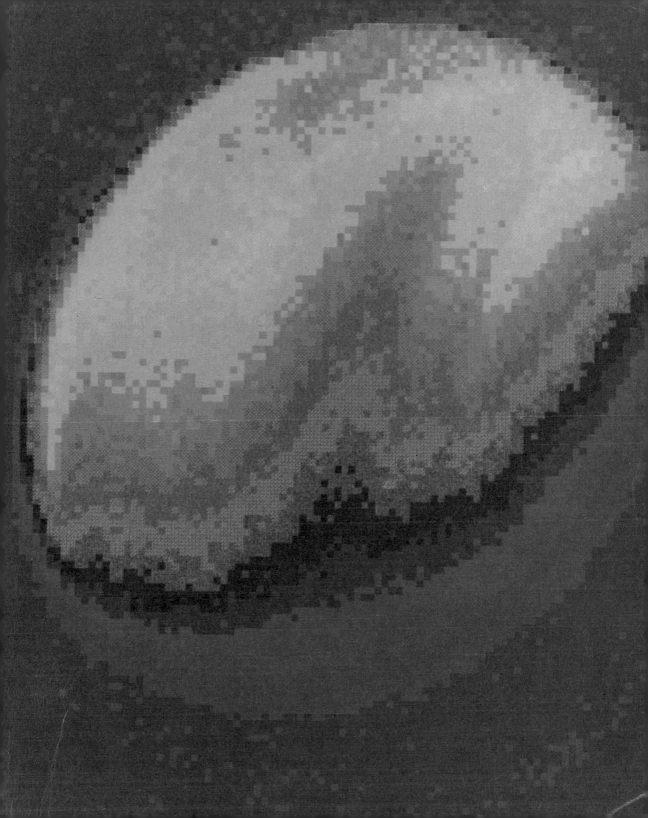

Data from *Pioneer Venus* shows that Venusian gravity is strongest over the planet's mountainous areas. Experts think young volcanic rocks from recent eruptions may be piled up in those highland regions. The pull of Venus's gravity, combined with the high concentrations of *sulfur dioxide* in its atmosphere, may mean that there are active volcanoes on Venus.

Venus does not seem to have a *magnetic field.* On Earth, a magnetic field makes it possible for a compass needle to point to the magnetic north pole no matter where the compass is placed.

Experts believe the heat in Earth's *outer core* and the speed of Earth's rotation set up electric currents. This combination gives Earth its mag-

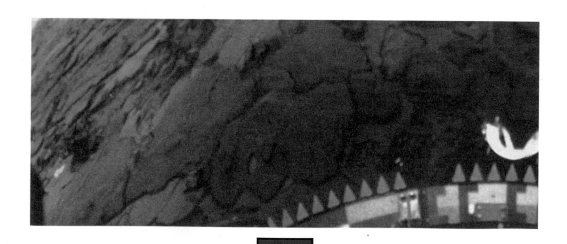

netic field. Venus, on the other hand, rotates slowly. Perhaps the hot liquid in its outer core does not move fast enough to set up electric currents. Without them, there is no magnetic field.

VENUS: FINDINGS

Even with all these new puzzles to solve, the radar did answer one of the scientists' oldest questions.

The Soviet probe *Venera 14* sent back these images of the rocky Venusian surface. The probe lasted less than an hour under the high-temperature surface conditions.

It told them that underneath the mysterious Venusian clouds lay mountains, volcanoes, and continent-sized landmasses. The images were too hazy for geologists to tell what forces had shaped them. But experts learned enough to say that the chemical composition of Venus is similar to the chemical composition of Earth.

Each planet has a *core* composed of iron and nickel. Each core has two parts: a solid *inner core* and a semiliquid outer core. This theory is based upon the measurements of two kinds of earthquake waves on Earth. Both kinds of waves pass through rock, but only one of them passes through liquid.

Scientists think that surrounding each core is a wide *mantle.* It is like a thick paste made of rocks that are so hot they bend and ooze. This plastic-like material moves all the time, carrying heat from the solid inner core, through its semiliquid outer core, toward the surface. Covering the mantle, like the bumpy rind of an orange, is a rocky crust.

PLATE TECTONICS

Experts who study plate tectonics want to know whether the crust of Venus is like Earth's crust.

They wonder if it is composed of thin, brittle, odd-looking shapes they call plates. If it is, they want to know how the plates on Venus behave.

They also want to investigate formations on Venus that resemble patterns crossing a vast submarine mountain range in the middle of the Atlantic Ocean, known as the Mid-Atlantic Ridge.

Beneath the ridge, plates are pulling away from each other. New materials from the mantle ooze up through the cracks, releasing a great deal of Earth's internal heat. On Earth, this new material also makes the seafloor spread. That makes the plates, upon which the continents float, drift farther and farther apart.

This might make it appear that Earth is expanding, but it is not. Plates that pull apart in one area just pile up in another. To see how this works, take three pieces of paper and line them up end to end. Pull one of the end papers and the middle paper apart. What happens to the third piece? It either ducks underneath the middle paper or flips up on top of it. That is what happens to the drifting plates.

Once in a great while, scientists can see the results of plates drifting. In Djibouti (pronounced dē-boō'-tē), East Africa, scientists are watching and measuring a giant crack they call a *rift* as it

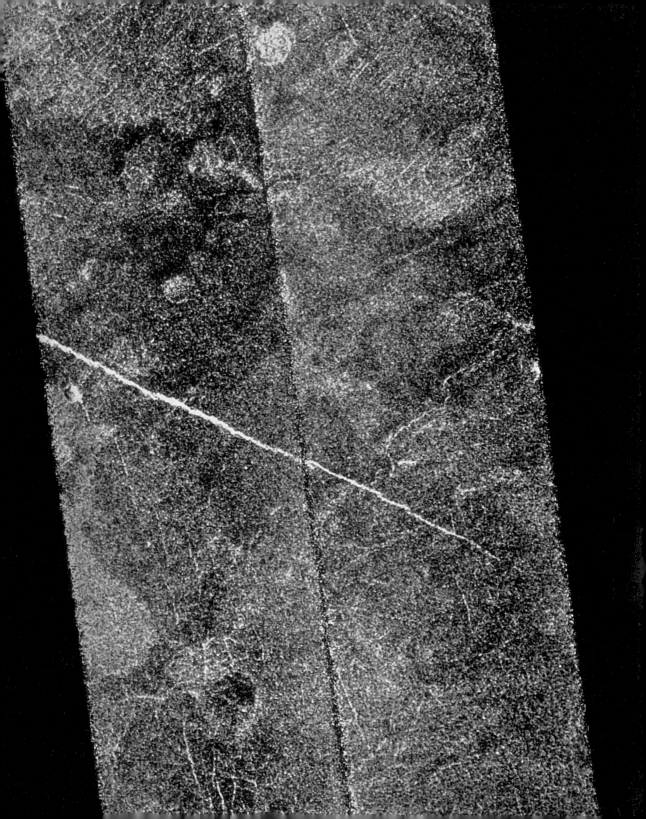

slowly gets deeper and wider. Geologists think that thousands of years from now, that opening will be our next ocean.

NAMING VENUSIAN LANDFORMS

Venus has a similar area called Diana Chasma. Scientists think it, too, may be a rift valley caused by the tectonic activity of two plates pulling apart.

Diana Chasma (named for the goddess of the hunt), and all the other landforms on Venus, have been named by the International Astronomical Union. This seventy-year-old group assigns titles and terminology to all the planetary bodies.

A mosaic image composed of two "image strips" of the Venusian surface obtained from the *Magellan* spacecraft. The bright line running downward from left to right is a fault zone cutting across volcanic plains.

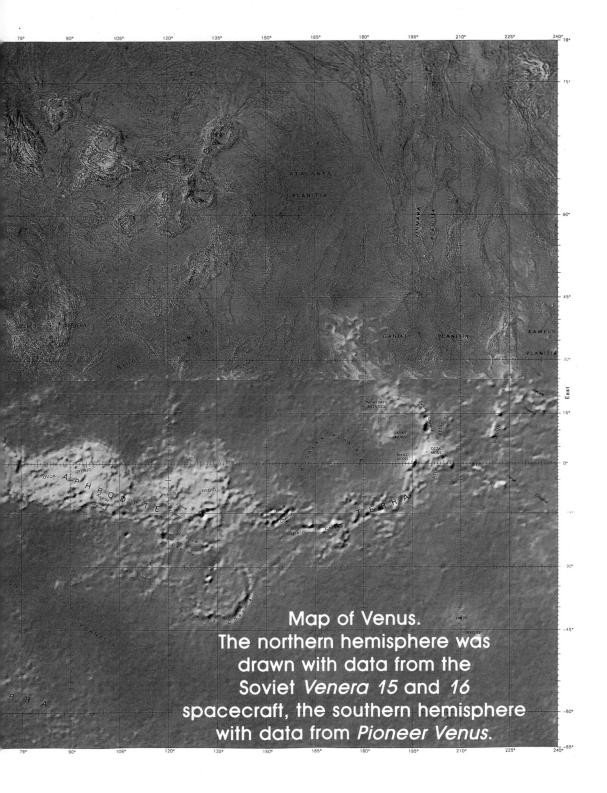

Map of Venus.
The northern hemisphere was
drawn with data from the
Soviet *Venera 15* and *16*
spacecraft, the southern hemisphere
with data from *Pioneer Venus.*

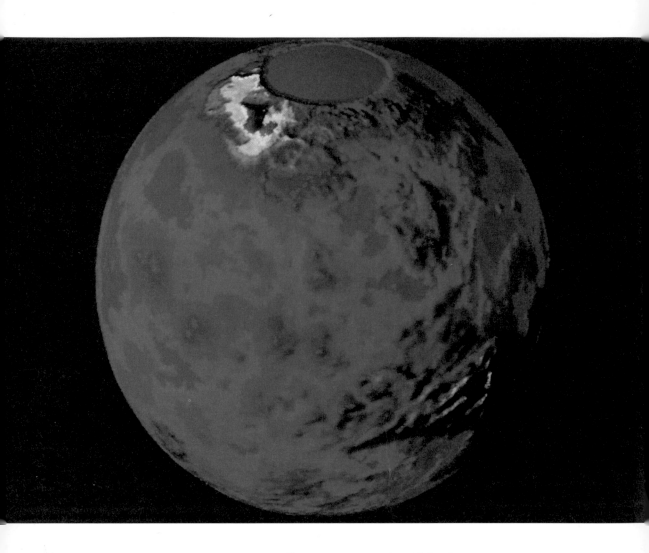

The green-yellow areas in this image
represent the two major continent-sized
landmasses of Venus, Ishtar (top left),
and Aphrodite (bottom right). Note that
the polar region has yet to be mapped.

One of its first tasks was to create a naming system for Venus. When women heard about the project, they wrote from all over the world. They wanted the features on Venus to be named for females. And so they are, except for one: Mt. Maxwell. It honors James Clerk Maxwell (1831–1879), whose mathematical formulas were responsible for interpreting all the early radar information from Venus: its size, rotation, and its major features.

The other landforms on Venus are named after the world's real or mythological women through all of history. Venus's two major continent-sized landmasses, Aphrodite and Ishtar, are named for Greek and Babylonian goddesses of love and beauty. Ishtar is about the size of Australia. Jutting up from its highlands is Mt. Maxwell. Scientists think it may be an active volcano. At 35,400 feet (10,800 m), it is one of the highest mountains in the solar system.

Aphrodite is larger, approximately the size of South America. It has two large mountainous areas at opposite sides of the continent. It also has the lowest depression on Venus, Diana Chasma.

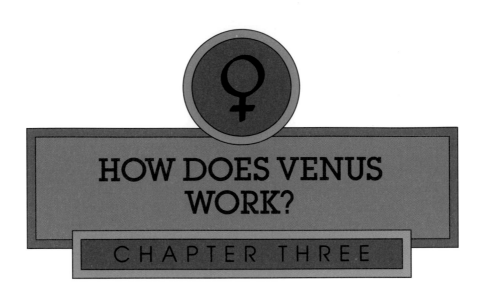

HOW DOES VENUS WORK?

CHAPTER THREE

EARTHQUAKES

On Earth, the movements of tectonic plates can cause earthquakes. Besides their rolling, shaking, and jerking motions, earthquakes can destroy buildings and break level land apart. At the *fault*, or break, rocks and earth on one side may slip sideways, up or down from rocks and earth on the opposite side.

Along the San Andreas Fault, which parallels the coast of California, the North American and Pacific plates rub against each other in a jerky motion, which is the reason California has so many earthquakes.

Sometimes the shoving is so great that one plate is rammed underneath another. That kind of tectonic activity often scrunches the land and pushes it upward. That is how mountains such as the Himalayas in Asia, the Alps in Europe, and the Rockies in North America were formed.

VOLCANOES

On Earth, the pushing of one plate under another can also cause volcanoes to erupt. That happens all around the edges of the Pacific Plate, from Alaska to Chile; from the Aleutian Islands to Japan, the Philippines, Indonesia, New Zealand, and the Hawaiian Islands. There are so many active volcanoes in the mountains of this area that *volcanologists,* scientists who study volcanoes, call the area the "Pacific Ring of Fire."

Other planets have volcanoes, too. Venus may have many. Whether they are active and whether they work the same way as volcanoes on Earth are questions scientists want answered. Some believe Venus may have forms of volcanic activity never seen on Earth.

Some believe that explosive eruptions on Venus may not be as spectacular as similar eruptions on Earth. The mountains they build may not

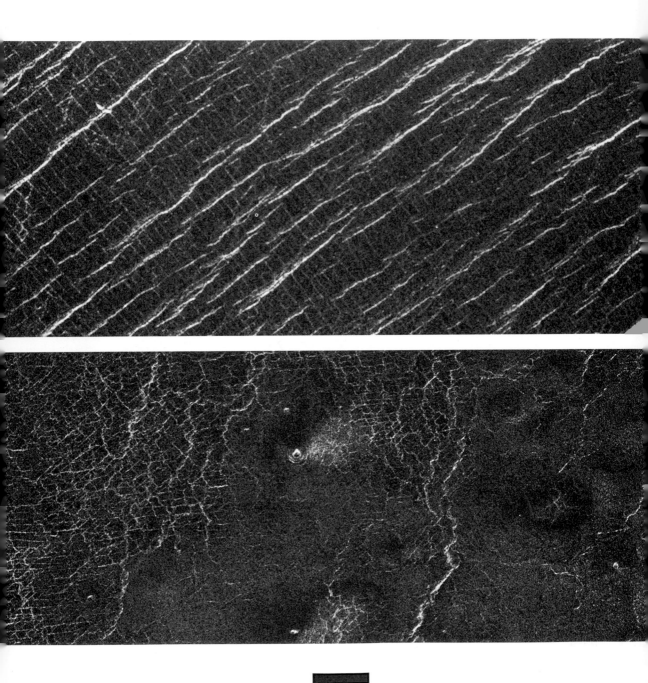

36

be very high. Scientists point to the many horizontal landmasses on the Venusian surface. They say the shapes may be the result of heat pushing up from inside the planet and high temperatures pressing down from outside. It is possible that the tremendous air pressure on Venus stops volcanic explosions altogether.

SHIELD VOLCANOES AND FLOOD BASALTS

Scientists who study planets, called *planetologists,* think that Venus and Earth have some similar landforms. Those experts think they have seen images of *flood basalts* and *shield volcanoes* on Venus.

Two *Magellan* radar images.
Above: Intersecting lines, thought
to represent faults or fractures,
in the Lakshmi region of Venus.
Below: Scientists believe this
image shows a volcanic crater
(center) surrounded by
deposits from volcanic
explosion plumes.

Shield volcanoes have gently sloping domes. They were built by *runny lava* that flowed out of low *vents,* or openings, on the mountains. Usually those mountains look flat and cover enormous areas, like Hawaii's Mauna Loa.

Flood basalts are the result of runny lava pouring out of cracks in the ground. This lava does not explode, it flows. Sometimes it covers hundreds, even thousands of square miles.

EROSION AND WEATHERING

On Earth, it takes hundreds of years for volcanoes and plate tectonics to build mountains. Even while the mountains are rising, *erosion* and *weathering* begin to wear them down and reshape them. Water, wind, and heat cause erosion and weathering on Earth. There is no water on Venus, hence no erosion. Weathering, however, may exist on Venus. It is probably slower and very different from what we see on Earth.

Wind on Venus's surface is thought to be slower than wind on Earth. Though experts think Venusian wind gets stronger as it rises, they have not seen the usual signs—no sand dunes, no piles of rubble strewn around the mountains. Without these clues, scientists believe that heat and corrosive gases are the only causes of weathering on Venus.

CRATERS

Besides seeing the mountains as they were before the effects of weathering and erosion, scientists hope to see unspoiled *craters* on Venus. There are *volcanic craters* called *calderas,* which are giant holes, in the mountains. They were blasted out by exploding volcanoes or formed by the collapse of *magma chambers.* There are also *impact craters.* These were gouged into the Venusian surface when meteorites smashed into the planet. The holes they made are rounder.

Planetologists think the more cratered a surface, the older it is. Even though Earth has been hit by meteorites in the past, scientists say it looks younger than Venus. Can it be that weathering, erosion, and constant tectonic activity on Earth have erased most of the craters' scars?

THE GREENHOUSE EFFECT

Think how hot the inside of a closed car gets on a sweltering day; if no one is around to open the windows, it just gets hotter and hotter. That is what has happened to the planet Venus. The dense clouds that always cover it are like the glass in the greenhouse and the windows in the closed car. "All the carbon dioxide (on Venus) stays in the at-

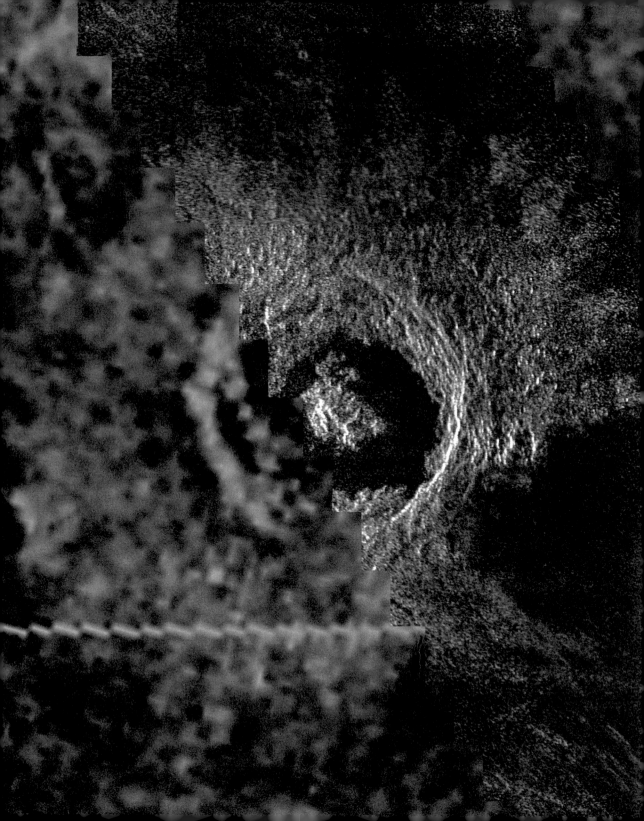

mosphere," JPL's Dr. R. Stephen Saunders says. The heat can get in but it cannot get out.

Venus is closer to the Sun, so it is understandable that it is hotter. It also gets twice the amount of radiation that Earth gets. Some scientists think Venus once had water but the planet's high temperatures boiled it away. They think that any water vapor left in the atmosphere broke up into oxygen and hydrogen. Oxygen is heavy, so it probably oxidized rocks on the Venusian surface. Hydrogen is lighter, so it probably escaped into space. But everyone agrees that now there is no water or water vapor in the Venusian atmosphere, just poisonous chemicals, such as sulfuric acid and carbon dioxide.

Golubkina, a crater on Venus, in an image created by combining photographs taken by *Magellan* and a Soviet Venera craft. The *Magellan* portion of the image (right), reveals the central peak, inner terraced walls, and smooth crater floor. The central peak is formed by the rebound of the floor after meteor impact.

Nothing can live or grow on Venus. Besides its searing surface temperature of almost 900° Fahrenheit, its atmospheric pressure is ninety times what it is on Earth. That is like being 2,500 to 3,000 feet (762 to 914 m) under the ocean.

SEEDING THE CLOUDS

Some experts talk about breaking up the carbon dioxide in Venus's clouds. Their plan is to seed the Venusian atmosphere with green plants from Earth. The plants would float on the clouds supported by balloons. Scientists predict that little by little the plants would use up some of the carbon dioxide in the clouds. This would produce small pockets of oxygen.

Experts think that some of the heat from Venus could escape through the pockets and stop or even reverse the *greenhouse effect*. Perhaps, they say, after hundreds of years Venus might even cool off.

Nobody knows yet how Venus became a runaway greenhouse. Nobody wants anything like that to happen on Earth. We are counting on the spaceship *Magellan* to teach us more about the greenhouse effect and how it can be reversed.

MOSAICS AND NOODLES AND SWATHS

The spacecraft *Magellan* was named after Ferdinand Magellan, a sixteenth-century Portuguese explorer. Magellan named the Pacific Ocean and mapped a route across it. Although he was killed on the voyage, his crew sailed on. They became the first men to circle the globe. Scientists think that the spacecraft *Magellan,* in mapping the planet Venus, will also change the world.

MAGELLAN'S RADAR

Magellan's primary mission (the reason it was sent to Venus) was to map up to 90 percent of the planet's surface. The spacecraft was programmed to

This photo of a portion of the Sahara Desert, taken with a radar similar to *Magellan*'s SAR, revealed a network of riverbeds 2.5 to 7 feet beneath the desert sands.

gather information three ways. Its *altimeter antenna* measures the height of the landforms it passes over. Its *radiometer* measures heat coming from the planet. Its *synthetic aperture radar (SAR)* locates landforms.

When *Magellan* is mapping, the SAR sends thousands of radar signals per second down through Venus's multilayered clouds. The strength of the signals and the length of time it takes for them to make the round trip to the surface and back are carefully recorded.

Signals that are short and bunched together mean that *Magellan* is approaching a landform. Signals that are longer and stretched out indicate that *Magellan* is leaving that same landform. The difference in the sounds is called the *Doppler effect*.

In order to use this technology properly, it was necessary to develop special computer processing on Earth. The new processing makes the SAR images of Venus ten times sharper than any images ever before received.

Imagine that you are a passenger on a spacecraft thirty-three million miles out in space. You are taking pictures of Earth. It probably wouldn't surprise you that you couldn't see Los Angeles at all. If you used the radar on the *Pioneer Venus*

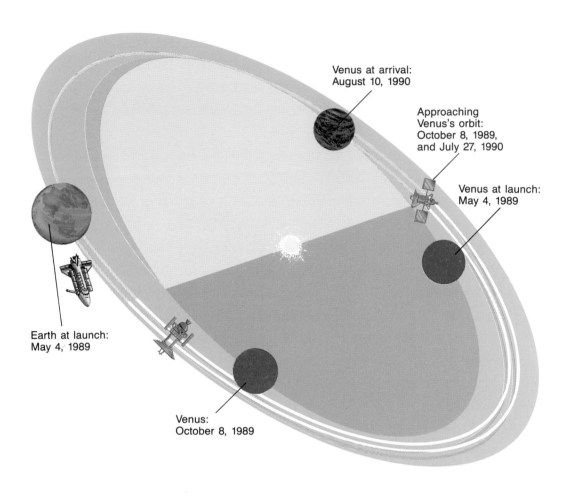

Venus at arrival:
August 10, 1990

Approaching
Venus's orbit:
October 8, 1989,
and July 27, 1990

Venus at launch:
May 4, 1989

Earth at launch:
May 4, 1989

Venus:
October 8, 1989

Magellan's fifteen-month voyage to Venus
in 1989-90. The spacecraft flew into
Venus's orbit, then back out to Earth's
before making her final approach of Venus.

spacecraft, you could see Los Angeles. It would look like a pencil dot. If you used the radar on *Magellan,* you could not only see Los Angeles, but the pencil dot would now represent Dodger Stadium.

Planetologists hope the *Magellan* radar's high resolution will enable them to see whether the planet has plate tectonics and whether there has been movement of the crustal plates.

SCIENTISTS' EXPECTATIONS

Volcanologists hope to see craters on Venus that are as they were when they were first formed. They want to know where the craters are, how many there are, and what shapes they have.

Since most volcanoes on Earth begin under-water, they are usually covered up. Volcanologists think the Venusian surface will show entire patterns of volcanoes and new crust formations. They want to know what motions cause the Earth to tremble and how new land develops.

Geologists hope to examine the amounts and kinds of lava on Venus. They expect it to give them clues about the thickness of the planet's crust and what materials are inside the planet.

If Venus had water at one time, scientists expect to find traces of the scars it left. They will be looking for the outlines of river basins, fluvial plains, river channels, and deltas.

This may sound impossible, but it is not. In 1981, SIR-A, a radar similar to the SAR, flew high above the Sahara Desert. There, it discovered an ancient network of riverbeds buried underneath the sand. Later, a team of scientists went to the area and dug up the sand in several locations. Experts found that long, long ago, there really had been a system of rivers about 2.5 to 7 feet (.08 m to 2.2 m) beneath the Sahara Desert sand.

MAGELLAN'S MAPPING

Magellan sweeps from Venus's north pole down toward its south pole, in an elliptical orbit between 155 and 1,300 miles (249 and 2,092 km) above the planet. On every sweep, *Magellan* collects data from a strip of Venus called a *swath.* Each swath covers a different area of the planet. At the same time, each swath slightly overlaps the swath taken on *Magellan's* previous orbit. A single swath represents an area 15 miles (24 km) wide and 10,000 miles (16,097 km) long.

A swath takes thirty-seven minutes to record. When *Magellan* is traveling to and from the far-

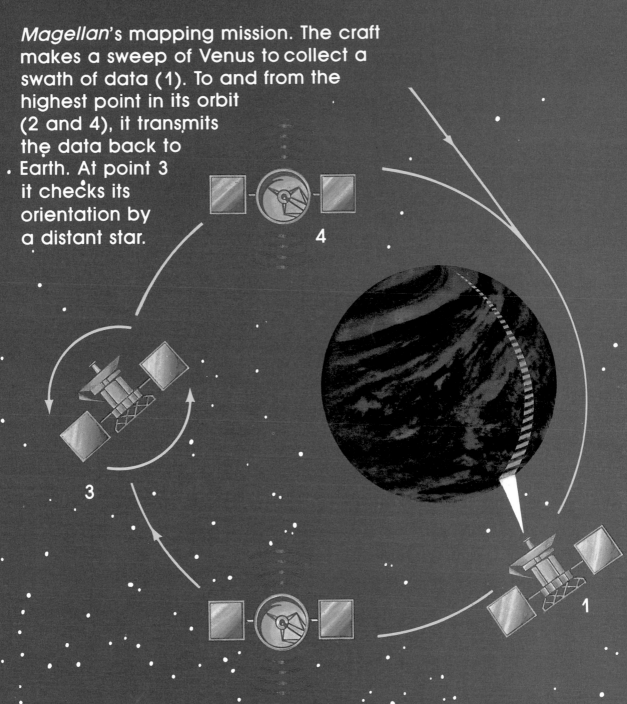

Magellan's mapping mission. The craft makes a sweep of Venus to collect a swath of data (1). To and from the highest point in its orbit (2 and 4), it transmits the data back to Earth. At point 3 it checks its orientation by a distant star.

thest point in its orbit, the spacecraft is pro-grammed to rewind its onboard tape recorders and turn toward Earth. *Magellan* then *dumps,* or sends back to Earth, all the stored data. After-ward, it again turns toward Venus and begins the cycle anew.

Magellan will make approximately 1,852 mapping swaths. It will take each swath from three to eleven minutes to reach one of three spe-cial receiving stations on Earth. One is in the Mojave Desert in California, one is near Madrid, Spain, and one is near Canberra, Australia. To-gether, they are known as the *Deep Space Net (DSN).* Twenty-four hours a day their giant anten-nas track every U.S. space mission.

NOODLES AND MOSAICS

From the DSN, the swaths of data are relayed in a stream of information called *noodles.* The noo-dles are sent to JPL, where they are processed.

As the noodles are collected they are pieced together to form a two-dimensional *mosaic,* a patchwork image of Venus. Areas of special in-terest will be processed into computer pictures.

The United States and the Soviet Union have shared information about Venus in the past. *Magellan*'s data will also be shared. Guest investigators, scientific specialists from the Soviet Union, England, France, Canada, and Australia, have been invited to the United States. Here, they will study and analyze the Venus mosaic. Copies of parts of the mosaic will also be sent to universities and laboratories throughout the world, where each tiny detail will be examined thoroughly.

SOVIET FINDINGS

Before 1990, there had been twenty U.S. and Soviet fly-bys, probes, and radar mappings of Venus. America's *Pioneer Venus* spacecraft found differing amounts of sulfur dioxide in the Venusian atmosphere. Such findings may mean that Venus has active volcanoes on its surface.

All of the Soviet Venera and Vega probes of the 1970s and early 1980s were crushed by Venus's high surface temperatures. Fortunately, seven of them lasted almost an hour. That was long enough to analyze air, soil, and rock samples and to take some photographs.

Those tests and pictures proved that there was no water and no water vapor on Venus, and no oxygen in Venus's air. It showed that rock and soil samples taken near the landing sites are composed mostly of basalt, as they are on Earth.

Venera 15 and *16* also discovered new kinds of

landforms. Soviet investigators call one of them *parquet,* or *tessera.* That is because their pattern of ridges and valleys look like inlaid wooden floor tiles.

Another new landform has large circular or oblong features that scientists call *coronae,* or *ovoids.* Experts disagree about their origin. Some say they may represent the scars of ancient impact craters. Others say they may have been formed by volcanoes or by activity inside the planet.

A third, probably of volcanic origin, is called a *spider.* Its markings look something like a gigantic spiderweb with a spider in the middle of it. About eighty of them have been discovered in the Venera images.

MAGELLAN AT VENUS

Magellan, the first spacecraft ever deployed from an orbiting shuttle, traveled 947,857,624 million miles in fifteen months; even though it often traveled faster than 75,000 miles an hour (the speed at which a jet airplane could fly from New York to Los Angeles in less than three minutes). It arrived at Venus, exactly as experts predicted, at 9:41:05 A.M., on August 10, 1990.

One of the most stunning images *Magellan* has sent us is this mosaic showing three large meteorite impact craters, separated by fractured plains, in the Lavinia region of Venus.

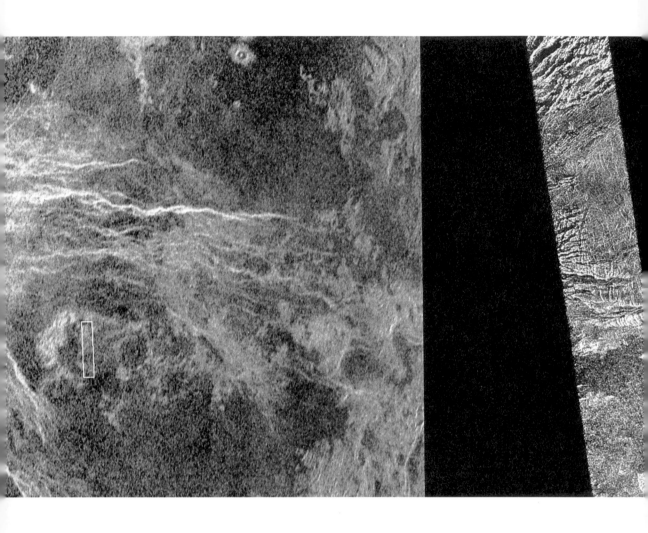

Note the fineness of detail in the
Magellan image (right) compared to the
highest-resolution Earth-based image (left).
Area shown (corresponding to the box)
is located in Beta Regio.

Noodles from *Magellan*'s first checkout orbits surprised scientists. From only 400 feet (120 meters), processed pictures clearly showed: major faults, a network of intersecting ridges and valleys called *tessera*, a multiple-ring circular feature of probable volcanic origin, Golubkina crater, small portions of Rhea Mons volcano, and a major volcanic upland called Beta Regio.

"Venus's geologic history seems more violent than I had expected," said JPL's Dr. Stephen Saunders. From all the faulting, "Venus quakes," unlike earthquakes, appear to have taken place over wide areas.

But in addition to the differences between Venus and Earth, Saunders identified such similarities as lava flows of varying ages like those on Hawaii and in Idaho's Snake River Plains; patterns of mountains and valleys resembling those of the Rocky Mountains; and Golubkina's extremely smooth floor, inner terraced walls, and central peak which are typical of large impact craters on Earth, the Moon, and Mars.

THE FUTURE

Shortly after *Magellan*'s first mapping test, and several times thereafter, *Magellan*'s on-board computers lost contact with Earth. Many possibilities were investigated, including electrical storms on Venus, light reflected from a star or the sun interfering with transmission, or software problems.

Magellan has enough fuel to last another twenty-five to thirty years, however, and eventually the spacecraft will send back to Earth more data than has been gathered by all previous U.S. planetary missions combined that will be enough to keep scientists busy for 100 years!

GLOSSARY

Altimeter antenna—An instrument whose radar signals determine the height of the landform directly below it.

Calderas—Volcanic craters.

Core—The innermost part of Earth, the Moon, and other terrestrial planets. Earth's core is composed of iron and nickel.

Corona—See *Ovoid*

Craters—Gigantic bowl-shaped holes in the surfaces of Earth, the Moon, and other terrestrial planets.

Crust—The thin, rocky, outermost layer of Earth, the Moon, and other terrestrial planets.

Deep Space Net (DSN)—Three special receiving stations around the world whose giant antennas track all U.S. space missions.

Doppler effect—Changes in sound frequencies that pinpoint the location of a certain object or landform.

Dump—Send back to Earth all the data collected on one sweep of Venus.

Fault—A break in the Earth's crust caused by earthquakes.

Field of gravity—The area around a planet in which an unseen force pulls the objects nearest to it toward the planet.

Flood basalt—The result of an eruption of runny lava, which is composed mostly of basalt. Flood basalts often spread over hundreds or even thousands of square miles.

Gravity—An unseen force that pulls objects toward the planet nearest to it.

Greenhouse effect—A term used to describe what happens when heat is trapped in Earth's atmosphere.

Impact craters—Giant bowl-shaped holes on the surfaces of Earth, the Moon, and other terrestrial planets, formed when struck by meteors.

Inner core—The solid center of Earth, the Moon, and other terrestrial planets.

Magma—Lava, when it is still inside a volcano.

Magma chambers—Areas somewhere in the mantle where melted rocks and gasses form pools of magma. Also called *magma reservoirs.*

Magnetic field—A combination of heat in the outer core of a planet and the speed of the planet's rotation that together makes a compass needle point to the magnetic north pole no matter where a compass is placed.

Mantle—The area between Earth's outer core and crust.

Mosaic—A two-dimensional image of Venus made by piecing together, and slightly overlapping, processed noodles.

Noodle—A stream of information.

Outer core—The area between Earth's inner core and its mantle.

Ovoid—A new type of circular or oblong landform on Venus discovered in Soviet *Venera 15* and *16* photographs. Also called corona.

Parquet—A new type of landform on Venus consisting of ridges and valleys, discovered in Soviet *Venera 15* and *16* photographs. Also called *tessera.*

Plates—Odd-shaped sections of Earth's crust upon which landmasses and oceans float.

Phases of Venus—The changing crescents of Venus, seen from Earth, as Venus orbits the Sun.

Radar—Radio signals that travel to an object and reflect signals from that object at the speed of light. An acronym of: RAdio Detection and Ranging.

Radiometer—An instrument that measures the amount of heat coming from a planet.

Retrograde—A backward motion; moving clockwise.

Rift—A land split where two sections of Earth's crust are pulling apart.

Runny lava—Consisting mainly of basalt, it pours out of volcanoes but does not explode.

SAR—Synthetic aperture radar. Radio signals that locate landforms.

Shield volcanoes—Built up from repeated eruptions of runny lava. These volcanoes have gently sloping domes and usually cover enormous areas.

Spider—A new type of landform resembling a spiderweb with a spider in the center of it, discovered on Venus in Soviet *Venera 15* and *16* photographs.

Sulfuric acid—A heavy, colorless, destructive acid found in Venus's cloud layer.

Swath—A single strip of data collected by *Magellan* as it orbits and maps Venus. A single swath represents an area 15 miles wide and 10,000 miles long.

Synthetic aperture radar—SAR, radio signals that locate landforms.

Tectonic—Another word for construction—like the construction of Earth's crust.

Tessera—Tile. A new type of landform discovered on Venus in Soviet *Venera 15* and *16* photographs. Also called parquet.

Vents—Openings on volcanic mountains through which lava flows.

Volcanic craters—Giant bowl-shaped holes on the surface of Earth, the Moon, and other terrestrial planets formed by volcanic explosions or the collapse of magma chambers.

FOR FURTHER READING

Asimov, Isaac. *Venus, Near Neighbor of the Sun.* New York: Lothrop, Lee & Shepard Books, 1981.

Bain, Iain. *Planet Earth Mountains and Earth Movements.* New York: The Bookwright Press, 1984.

Bramwell, Martyn. *Mountains.* New York: Franklin Watts, 1986.

Bramwell, Martyn. *Volcanoes and Earthquakes.* New York: Franklin Watts, 1986.

Gallant, Roy A. *National Geographic Picture Atlas of Our Universe.* Washington, D.C.: National Geographic Society, 1980.

Gallant, Roy A. *The Planets, Exploring the Solar System.* New York: Four Winds Press, 1982.

Hansen, Rosanna, and Robert A. Bell. *My First Book of Space.* New York: Little Simon Books, 1985.

Hunt, Garry E., and Patrick Moore. *The Planet Venus.* London: Faber and Faber, 1983.

Jackson, Joseph H., and John H. Baumert. *Pictorial Guide to the Planets.* New York: Harper & Row, 1981.

Lauber, Patricia. *Journey to the Planets.* New York: Crown, 1987.

Nourse, Alan E. *The Giant Planets.* New York: Franklin Watts, 1982.

Reigot, Betty P. *A Book about Planets.* New York: Scholastic Book Services Inc., 1981.

Taylor, G. Jeffrey. *Volcanoes in Our Solar System.* New York: Dodd, Mead & Company, 1983.

Vogt, Gregory. *Mars and the Inner Planets.* New York: Franklin Watts, 1982.

INDEX